Crystal Healing

Fact or fiction?
Real or imaginary?

Why not judge for yourself!

Robert W. Wood D.Hp
(Diploma in Hypnotherapy)

Rosewood Publishing

First published in U.K. 2002
By Rosewood Publishing
P.O. Box 219, Huddersfield,
West Yorkshire HD2 2YT

www.rosewood-gifts.co.uk

Robert W Wood D.Hp
Asserts the moral right to be identified
As the author of this work

Copy-editing
Margaret Wakefield BA (Hons) London
www.euroreportage.co.uk

Cover photograph by
Andrew Caveney BA (Hons)
www.andrewcaveneyphotography.co.uk

Cover and layout re-designed by
AJ Typesetting
www.ajtype.co.uk

Printed in Great Britain by
Delta Design & Print Ltd
www.deltaleeds.co.uk

ISBN 978-0-9532930-5-6   BK6

Nature's crystals: a fascinating, wonderful world of shapes. Can there be a more spectacular sight than frozen water, especially when it's in the form of a crystal snowflake?

Crystal healing, fact or fiction?

Everybody's heard stories about crystal healing. There was the woman who was given a crystal to help her bad knee and then found, to her amazement, that her knee miraculously got better. Or people who can't sleep, who find that placing an Amethyst under their pillow seems to make them sleep like logs. Would you believe headaches can just seem to vanish? That'll be a Rose Quartz. Women becoming pregnant after years of trying - ask them how, and they'll say it was a Moonstone. Eyesight improving - that'll be Obsidian Snowflake. Memory improving - Rhodonite. Need to boost your confidence? - then try a Tiger's Eye, a beautiful stone from South Africa.

You could bring back the joys of spring with a Sodalite; and if you place a Sodalite with a Rhodonite in a glass of water, it produces the 'elixir of life', said to rejuvenate and produce youthfulness. Aches and pains? Then what you need is a Rose Quartz and a Hematite combined. It's said they work wonders on aches and pains. Maybe you would like a little 'peace of mind'? Then try Green Aventurine, Rose Quartz and Rhodonite. Not feeling too good? then the 'Healer' could be just what the doctor ordered: Carnelian, Red Jasper and Rock Crystal. And there are many more, so whatever the problem, there'll be a crystal that can help.

For many years I have researched, studied and even demonstrated crystal healing in front of well over one hundred thousand people. I have read books, reports and articles. I have used and searched the Internet. I have seen and heard so many stories about healing crystals. In fact I have served my apprenticeship 'out in the field', so to speak, in front of hundreds of groups representing lots of organisations, with people coming from all walks of life. So what are we to make of all this? Is it real, or could we take it all with a pinch of salt and ignore it? I think it's not whether crystals work, but how do they work?

One of my observations over the years has got to be that men are more cynical than women. However, there is a kind of hush that settles down over the men once I am into my presentation. I think it's because the men are surprised to hear, in words, what women seem to already know; and it's something women seem to have a feel for intuitively. Women seem to accept crystal healing quite easily. On the other hand, academics find it very difficult, if not almost impossible, to accept a simple, esoteric, new-age philosophy. Many books written by academics seem to find it difficult to comprehend the simplistic, holistic approach to healing with crystals. My point is this: in the end you will have to make up your own mind. I suggest you keep an open mind.

Can't see the obvious?
Here's a little story to make my point:
Sherlock Holmes and Dr. Watson go camping. During the night, Holmes wakes his friend. "Watson, look up at the sky and tell me, what do you see?" And Watson says: "I see a million stars." Holmes asks, "What does that tell you?" The good doctor thinks about it and says: "Theologically, I can see that God is all powerful. Astronomically, it tells me there are a million galaxies. Astrologically, I observe that Saturn is in Leo. Meteorologically, I suspect tomorrow will be a beautiful day. Horologically, I deduce that it is 2.30am. What does it tell you, Holmes?" "Watson, my dear friend," said the great detective, "it tells me someone has stolen our tent."

Ask an academic if he or she believes in God, and here you will find your first problem: when they ask you to define what you mean by the word 'God'. You'll move into a world of semantics and miss the importance of a simple understanding. It doesn't get any easier when you understand that there is more than one truth. For example, you could ask one person to take a ride on a big dipper at the fun fair, and another to watch. Then see if they can both describe 'a big dipper' to someone else who doesn't have a clue as to what one is. Although they would be describing the same ride, they will give two different versions. It wouldn't even matter if you put them both onto the ride at the same time; you will still get two different versions. Over the years I have come across many people who are walking around, who will swear blind that a crystal or crystal healer cured them of whatever problems, illness or troubles they had. So whilst many are in denial, the rest are witnessing miracles that sometimes just beggar belief. Here's food for thought: *today is a gift*; that's why it's called *the present*.

Divided opinions.

When it comes to crystal healing, it's true to say that there are divided opinions. These range from the total non-believers to those who do believe, leaving the majority of us firmly in the middle, not knowing what to believe. The author of this book started out thinking it would probably all be nonsense, just like having fairies at the bottom of the garden. (Sorry, if you believe in fairies.) But I quickly learned it might not be nonsense, and in fact I now firmly believe that for many, under certain circumstances, crystal healing actually does seem to work. You will be the judge and jury. First let me present some interesting points of view - but do remember that it's you who will decide in the end.

To be fair, if the claims made by some were true - that crystals, lucky charms, amulets and healing stones are so effective - then common sense should tell us that nobody would be ill or emotionally upset ever again. Everybody would be wearing or carrying their own range of crystals around with them, because they would have discovered their very own panacea. Some could argue that because so many people do wear gemstones, crystals, lucky charms and amulets, they must work; or why else would people wear them? A simple answer could be that people hope they'll work, or even that they are wearing them just as a fashion item because, quite simply, they like them.

Is there a hidden code?

What if there is another explanation? What if it's not the stones or crystals after all, but a belief in them? And if this were true, then the healing mechanism would have to be triggered more from something within, rather than from without. Jesus Christ, the most famous of all healers, often spoke in a coded language before he performed a healing. Here are just a few examples - see if you can spot the code.

"Go! It will be done just as you believed it would," and his servant was healed at that very hour.   *Matthew 8 -13*

Then he touched their eyes and said, "According to your faith will it be done to you."   *Matthew 9 -29*

"If you have faith as small as a mustard seed, you can say to this mountain, move from here to there, and it will move. Nothing will be impossible for you."   *Matthew 17 - 20*

5

(Incidentally, I once moved a mountain. I have a friend who introduces me as 'the only man he knows who moved a mountain'. You'll have to read my book 'Discover Why Crystal Healing Works' for the full story; but all the same principles that I used are here in this book.)

"If you believe, you will receive whatever you ask for in prayer."
Matthew 21- 22

"If you can," said Jesus. "Everything is possible for him who believes." Immediately the boy's father explained, "I do believe; help me overcome my unbelief!"   *Mark 9 - 23*

"Daughter, your faith has healed you."   *Luke 8 - 48*

Hearing this, Jesus said to Jairus, "Don't be afraid; just believe, and she will be healed."   *Luke 8 - 50*

Are you getting the idea? And no, I'm not getting religious; it's just that if you can understand the code, you can start to understand 'healing'. I am not asking you to abandon your own powers of discrimination or personal intuitions in favour of a blind belief. Genuine knowledge and wisdom does not come from gullibility, but it comes from a deep questioning within, until the seeker has genuinely found his or her own answers.

Mother Nature.
In the past, man seems to have lived more in peace and harmony with Mother Nature and easily accepted earth's abundant treasures. You could say, man's first medicine chest was provided by Mother Earth in the form of herbs, flowers and fruits, crystals, minerals and rocks.

We have advanced so far with technology and scientific achievement today, that it almost seems unreal, just how far we have travelled and in such a short period of time. One minute you're reading science fiction comics of men going to the moon and thinking it'll never happen, then the next minute Neil Armstrong steps down from the lunar module of Apollo 11 on July 21, 1969, to become the first man to set foot on the moon, saying those immortal words, "That's one small step for a man; one giant leap for mankind." The effects that we now enjoy because of science have been of such enormous value and benefit to us all, that we may be guilty of being in such awe of it all that we may find ourselves forgetting the past, our roots.

From the previous chapter on the advancement of science, now read the following introduction to a book written by a man called Thomas Nicols. He was a learned man, a scholar and a translator, but he couldn't understand why his fellow scholars believed that various precious stones had supernatural, mystical powers. In 1652, at Jesus College, Cambridge, Thomas Nicols produced his book on Lapidary, a guide to Gemstones and their mysterious powers. Isaac Newton was only 10 years of age at the time and would, 35 years later, from the same college, publish his theory of universal gravitation - knowledge that the Apollo space flights relied on.

A Lapidary or The History of Pretious Stones
With cautions for the undeceiving of all those that deal
with Pretious Stones
by Thomas Nicols. Sometime of Jesus Colledge in Cambridge.
Printed by Thomas Buck Printer to the Universitie 1652
Surely, we live not in the most unknowing times of the world, nay, never was this part of the World fuller of knowledge than now it is wherein many are blest with excellent gifts and endowments by which they are enabled to enquire more thoroughly into the nature and causes of things.

Remembering who we are and where we have come from will help us to marry the valid 'old' knowledge to the 'new'. This will help us to gain a deeper understanding of ourselves, and to be in contact with our inner 'knowing'. With this thought in mind, if we study mankind from as far back as the days of the legendary lost city of Atlantis and the ancient Mayan and Hebrew civilisations, including native American as well as far Eastern cultures, we will find that throughout these ages, gemstones and crystals have been used in spiritual rituals, as aids to help with physical healing, and to help reduce stress and anxiety.

The road to Damascus.
When I first came across gemstone and crystal healing, I really thought this was more of a wind-up, put about by a few hippies who could only be described as crackpots. To be fair, they didn't do their cause any good by always looking spaced-out and saying, 'Peace, man!' If, like me, this is how you think, or if you think gemstone crystals are only lumps of rock, then all I ask is that you open your mind to other possibilities. If you had told me in 1993, when I first started my research, that I would become a strong advocate for crystal healing, then I would not have believed it.

In America there are surgeons who believe that a patient's convalescence is reduced by as much as a third when crystals are around during surgery. Although these surgeons admit they don't know why this should be, they accept it as a fact and always make sure that there are crystals in the operating theatre. Hospitals throughout the world - certainly the more enlightened ones - have taken note of the apparent therapeutic power of crystals; and so crystals can often be found at and around various points in hospitals.

Warning.

Do not accept blindly what you are told. I never have. Always verify for yourself. If you can, check the results that have been obtained by others who have used crystals. I personally have seen, heard and experienced some amazing stories regarding gemstone and crystal healing. I think for you, the reader, we will need to go to a deeper level of understanding. We need to build a case. We need to 'put some meat onto the bones'.

A deeper level.

Quartz Crystals and Gemstones have always been highly prized for their beauty, and also for their renowned healing and spiritual properties. They have been associated with healers, shamans, priests, spiritual seekers and many others who have all used these so-called 'special powers'. Science has yet to discover what is actually going on during crystal healing, and only by trying out a healing system for ourselves are we able to judge its worth. It may have surprised you to find that real changes are clearly felt, and lasting benefits are clearly gained, by many participants who have used crystals.

A very interesting fact about crystals is that they grow, and continue to grow until all the free atoms are arranged. A crystal may have remained the same for thousands or even millions of years, but crystals do actually grow in the ground in a matrix (this is a rock in which fossils, pebbles etc are embedded). Did you know that the most common element on earth is oxygen? And the second most common is silicon? So it won't be a surprise to find the most common of crystals is silicon quartz, a crystal that grows from the combination of silicon and oxygen. It's this crystal that they use in computers; that's why they say computer chips come from 'Silicon Valley'. Another more popular name for silicon quartz is rock crystal. You won't believe where you'll find quartz crystal these days - it's as if the oldest (quartz) is underpinning the newest (computers). Without quartz crystal we would still be in the dark ages.

A little science.

Quartz crystals absorb, use and store energy, and mature just like anything else in existence that we consider to be 'alive'. When subjected to outside forces such as light, pressure, heat or electricity, quartz crystals quickly restore themselves to their original internal stability. This stability is the quality that makes them so important in modern day technology.

We find crystals are used in watches - you must have heard of 'quartz watches'. Put on a CD player and you will have activated a sound system that uses a laser to read tiny pits and flat spots from a plastic coated metal disc. That laser uses a ruby crystal and this explains why the laser is red.

We can find crystals being used as switching and regulating devices in engines - engines that power everything from cars to space shuttles. Modern car radios use a transistor made from a silicon quartz crystal. So we are using crystals every day in the form of computer chips, liquid crystal displays, transistors, clocking devices ... and there are many more.

Colour: When other factors in nature become involved, such as natural inclusions or background radiation, then the characteristics of the quartz start to change enough for it to appear coloured or smoky. This factor very cleverly links crystals to their best use - for healing - because colour is used as a primary identification for gemstones and crystals. Amazingly, if a few atoms from another element become included within the lattice structure of the quartz molecules whilst the crystal is forming, or if another mineral crystallises within the quartz as it grows, it becomes distorted. This distortion helps to explain why there are so many coloured varieties of quartz.

For example, if iron is around and near to rock crystal when it's forming, then the effect is that it changes colour to Amethyst. That's what Amethyst is: rock crystal that's been 'distorted' by iron being too near to it when forming. It's like Rose Quartz. This has traces of magnesium and titanium and the effect created is a lovely pink crystal quartz.

Colour therapy.

To reach a deeper understanding of crystal healing, you will find it useful if we now explore colour therapy. Colour therapy, like gemstones and crystals, can be an effortless system of treatment that seems to help with illness, pain and tiredness. It can help us to look and feel younger and enable us to enjoy life with more energy, vigour and vitality - all this being achieved by simply using the mind to 'experience' colours. Our brain governs the healing and well-being process in our bodies. Indian yoga has identified seven energy centres - the 'Chakra' system - which must all be balanced for good health. What we are interested in here is energy - the healing energy.

More colour science.

Colour is a function of light. It is determined by the frequency of the light wave as observed by the human eye. The visible light spectrum goes from the lowest frequency, red, to the highest, violet. This spectrum is, in order: Red, Orange, Yellow, Green, Blue, Indigo and Violet. My way of remembering it when I was at school was: Richard Of York Gained Battles In Vain. (In case you didn't know, these are the seven colours of the rainbow, in the right order. Just take the first letter of each word and it corresponds to the first letter of each different colour of the rainbow.)

Mankind's effort to heal with light is as old as recorded history. The foundation of modern colour therapy rests with seventeenth-century scientists including Sir Isaac Newton (1642-1727) and his famous prism tests. He was the first to show that 'white light' is a mixture of all colours of the visible spectrum. He proved that when white light was passed through a glass prism it produced a seven-colour band, or a rainbow. When the seven-colour band was passed through a reversed prism, the colours re-combined to form white light again.

Others have taken this work further, and quite successfully explored colours and their effects in healing. Gemstones and crystals are easily identified by their colour; and this gives us a general guide to the frequencies on which they operate, and a link with their energy. Here's a theory: when you absorb colour energy it travels, via the nervous system, to the part of the body that needs it. (You'd think I was talking about painkillers.) Each body has its own optimum state of well-being and is constantly seeking ways to maintain or restore a balanced state. This explains 'cravings': it's the body's way of correcting imbalances, and compensating for any dietary deficiencies.

Healing energy - frequencies.

One of the characteristics of energy can be colour, and when measured, it's measured by its 'frequency'. The body also has 'frequencies' of energy waves. Some have been accurately measured by Western science; some haven't. However, just because science hasn't figured out how to measure them all, this doesn't mean they don't exist. Crystal therapy makes use of this energy system within the body. So in crystal healing, one of the first things to consider is the colour frequency.

There are specific areas of the body that are main centres for the flow of energy. In Sanskrit, they're called Chakras. (Sanskrit is an ancient language of India - in fact it is the oldest recorded member of the Indo branch of the Indo-European family of languages.) These energy centres correspond to frequencies, from low to high.

The lowest frequency energy centre is the first Chakra, and this is at the base of the spine. The next six are located in order, starting at the reproductive organs; then the navel area; the heart; the base of the throat; the brow; and finally at the crown of the head. The colours that represent these Chakras are roughly the frequencies that represent red to violet - lowest to highest.

So we are now establishing a very basic rule of thumb for the use of gemstones and crystals. Deep red stones such as Jasper or deeper Rose Quartz would resonate with the lower Chakras; and violet to clear, represented by Amethyst and Rock Crystal, would be associated with the higher ones.

My own research.

Years ago now, when I first started researching into the mysteries surrounding gemstones and crystals, I had chosen Red Jasper for the star sign Aries. You'll have to read my book 'Discover Why Crystal Healing Works' for a fuller explanation, but briefly - I wanted to find an authentic list of birthstones. I read and researched many different sources of information, and eventually decided to take the 'mean average', mainly because all my sources seemed to be saying something different. No two of the lists I was researching were saying the same thing. So I thought that if the majority were saying that Red Jasper was the stone for Aries, then that was good enough for me. This was how I acquired my unique list of twelve birthstones.

Gemstones Crystals and the Bible.

In my early days of research I used to pass around baskets full of Tumblestones, and I asked my audience to pick out a stone they liked. I was trying to establish whether there was a connection between birthstones and ourselves. I didn't think there would be; but to my amazement it seemed that there was, because many people seemed to pick out their own birthstone. Sometimes as many as 70% did. I also researched into connections between gemstones or crystals and the Bible, because a friend had told me that the gemstones and crystals I was researching could be found there.

Amazingly I seemed to find information was starting to flood in from all kinds of sources. Some seemed, at the time, very strange. I found people sent me information through the post, especially after they had heard me give my talk. They would write and say things like, "I hope this will help in your research". It felt as if I was being sent pieces of a jigsaw, and although at the time it felt odd it's surprising just how well all those pieces seem to have fitted together.

I noticed that passages from books were starting to stand out - but the strangest of all was when a Bible I was looking at seemed to open up and I was drawn to a story in Exodus (28 -15) relating to twelve stones. Strange, because at the time I was engaged in trying to find twelve authentic birthstones.

It became even stranger when, on the same day that I came across this story in Exodus, I found myself being drawn to a story in the New Testament entitled 'A New Jerusalem' (Revelation 21-19). When you consider that there are nearly one thousand four hundred pages in my Bible, with only two lists of twelve stones anywhere, and I seemed somehow to have found both lists on the same day, it is even more mystifying.

Was this a coincidence, or what? Curiously, this other list of twelve stones representing a New Jerusalem said that the first foundation was a Jasper. This was the same stone I had chosen for the birth sign Aries, which can be called the first foundation in Astrology and is the first one described in the Chakras.

Revelation 21-19

The sixth foundation of this New Jerusalem was Carnelian; the sixth star sign in astrology is Virgo, and its stone is a Carnelian. If ever the pieces of a jigsaw came together, they were doing so now! The twelfth and final foundation was Amethyst; in astrology, the last is Pisces. The birthstone selected was the same: Amethyst. And to cap it all, in the colours of the Chakra the last one, and the highest colour which is visible to the eye, is violet - Amethyst.

Colour therefore has proved to be a very important consideration in the concept of crystal healing. Now whilst colour may be important, other factors are too, because gemstones and crystals have an evolutionary history as well: that is, each stone or crystal over the years has attracted its own unique kind of 'providence'.

One of the qualities that typifies traditional healing arts, alternative therapies, etc, is the respect for the holistic nature of our existence: that the whole may be greater than the sum of its parts. You cannot work with the body and ignore the mind. The surgeon can repair an ulcer but the wise man looks for the reason behind the illness.

Healing Energy.

The healing energy which I mentioned earlier is not isolated. It is connected with the energy that is in all things. We are a part of a holistic event: the Universe.

One of the defining characteristics of traditional alternative therapies is the respect for, and awareness of, our natural healing energy - the life force built within. In Chinese it's known as 'chi'. The Ayuruedic system, handed down through 7,500-year-old Vedic texts of India, defines three basic energies: pitta, vata and kapha. The Christians refer to the Father, Son and Holy Spirit. The indigenous tribe of the Kalahari, in South Africa, refer to the healing power of nature as 'num'. There is not an ancient culture you can think of that doesn't acknowledge this natural connection with healing energy. So - healing energy, we now know, has certain characteristics. Learn how to acknowledge, honour and use this energy; for it is the key to healing. Gemstones and Crystals are an important part of that key. Use them.

And finally ..

The phone rang. "Can I get a piece of Amethyst?" the woman asked. "My friend heard you speak last week and you told her that maybe an Amethyst under her pillow would help her sleep. So she bought one, and ever since she's been sleeping like a log." It's nice when you get a call giving positive feedback. The woman went on to tell me that her friend had thought the first night might have just been a coincidence - but not the second or third. In fact, two of her friends who had bought Amethysts were both experiencing the same, so she had rung for an Amethyst to help her sleep.

A similar call, this time from a man: Could he have another set of healing crystals? He had bought the 'Healer' for his wife, who hadn't enjoyed good health for many years. He couldn't explain it, but she seemed to have got a kind of 'second wind' and was feeling much better than she had for a long time; and she wanted another set for a friend.

When I demonstrate crystal healing, I simply pass around a Rose Quartz and Hematite (it's said they work wonders on aches and pains). The audience then can judge for themselves. There is a point when I'll often say, "If anybody's got a headache at this moment in time then you'll find it will go." You wouldn't believe the number of people who will come over to me afterwards and say that if they hadn't experienced it for themselves, they would never have believed it - but the headache that they had come in with had actually gone.

There was a woman in York who had the same story of her headache going, and she decided to buy a special pair of sterling eardrops that we make using Rose Quartz and Hematite. She was hoping they might help as she had been suffering for a while from headaches. Three months later I saw her again in York at another display and she took great delight in showing me that she was still wearing her eardrops. She then said, "You won't believe this, but I haven't had a headache since that day."

The following information may help: Find the crystal that best suits you. Clean it - it's called cleansing. Connect with it - that means knowing where it is at all times. Then imagine the desired effect you'd like from it. Then imagine how you would feel if you achieved it - that is, energise it; and then believe. Just as Jesus said: Believe, and it will be yours. You've nothing to lose in trying, but everything to gain. Crystals have a part to play in everyone's lives. Feel free to experiment; but most of all, have fun!

The following information is a fluid interpretation from many sources. Any information given in this book is not intended to be taken as a replacement for medical advice. Any person with a condition requiring medical attention should consult a qualified doctor or therapist.

RED JASPER A powerful healing stone. Can help those suffering from emotional problems; its power to give strength and console such sufferers is well known. Good for: kidneys, bladder. Improves the sense of smell.

ROSE QUARTZ Healing qualities for the mind. Gives help with migraine and headaches. Good for: spleen, kidneys and circulatory system. Coupled with Hematite, works wonders on aches and pains throughout the body.

BLACK ONYX Can give a sense of courage, and helps to discover truth. Instils calm and serenity. Good for: bone marrow, relief of stress.

MOTHER OF PEARL Aptly dubbed the sea of tranquillity. Calms the nerves. Good for: calcified joints, digestive system.

TIGER EYE The 'confidence stone'. Inspires brave but sensible behaviour. Good for: liver, kidneys, bladder. Invigorates and energises.

CARNELIAN A very highly-evolved healer. Good for: rheumatism, depression, neuralgia. Helps regularise the menstrual cycle.

GREEN AVENTURINE Stabilises through inspiring independence. Acts as a general tonic. Good for: skin conditions; losing anxiety and fears.

RHODONITE Improves the memory; reduces stress. Good for: emotional trauma, mental breakdown; spleen, kidneys, heart and blood.

SODALITE Imparts youth and freshness. Calms and clears the mind. When combined with Rhodonite, can produce the 'Elixir of Life'.

OBSIDIAN SNOWFLAKE A powerful healer. Brings insight and understanding, wisdom and love. Good for: eyesight, stomach and intestines.

BLUE AGATE Improves the ego. A stone of strength and courage; a supercharger of energy. Good for: stress, certain ear disorders.

AMETHYST Aids creative thinking. Relieves insomnia when placed under pillow. Good for: blood pressure, fits, grief and insomnia.

HEMATITE A very optimistic inspirer of courage and magnetism. Lifts gloominess. Good for: blood, spleen; generally strengthens the body.

ROCK CRYSTAL Enlarges the aura of everything near to it and acts as a catalyst to increase the healing powers of other minerals. Good for: brain, soul; dispels negativity in your own energy field.

MOONSTONE Gives inspiration and enhances the emotions. Good for: period pain and kindred disorders, fertility and childbearing.

Power Gems.

Now here is a list of the most popular Power Gems, this time taking the desired effect, rather than the gemstones and crystals, as our starting point. Using our unique knowledge, we have created the following combinations from the 15 gemstones and crystals previously listed. For example, someone wanting to know the luckiest stones can look at 'Good Luck'. To find out the most powerful healing crystals, then look at 'Healer'. If you want the stones best suited to everyday ailments, then 'To Remove Aches & Pains' are the ones for you. Feeling under the weather? - then try 'To Lift Depression'; or if you're trying to lose weight or give up smoking, then try 'For Willpower'.

This range has been designed so that you don't have to guess which stones do what. In this day and age, some may take all this as no more than a little fun; but remember, years ago they didn't have chemists, and this is what people used: gemstones and crystals.

The most powerful combination of crystals discovered for healing:
HEALER - Carnelian, Red Jasper and Rock Crystal.

Three of the best-known Gemstones for attracting Good Luck:
GOOD LUCK - Obsidian Snowflake, Green Aventurine and Moonstone.

To capture 'stillness in movement', to attract harmony and tranquillity:
PEACE OF MIND - Green Aventurine, Rose Quartz and Rhodonite.

Stones and crystals to help us acquire willpower:
FOR WILLPOWER - Rose Quartz, Black Onyx and Rock Crystal.

Combined to create the most imaginative aphrodisiac. Very sensuous:
ADULTS ONLY - Rose Quartz, Amethyst and Carnelian.

Help to ease aches and pains including headaches and tensions:
TO REMOVE ACHES & PAINS - Rose Quartz, Hematite and Rock Crystal.

To preserve youth and retard the ageing process:
ELIXIR OF LIFE - Rhodonite and Sodalite.

Gemstones to help boost energy and vitality, to help invigorate:
ENERGY BOOSTER - Carnelian, Amethyst and Rock Crystal.

Designed for that special purpose, to reach a deeper level of mind:
IMAGINE - Rose Quartz, Amethyst and Green Aventurine.

To help nature along when starting a family:
FERTILITY - Moonstone, Rose Quartz and Rock Crystal.

See your local stockist for any Gemstones and Crystals mentioned in this publication. However, if you are having difficulty in obtaining any of the stones mentioned, we do offer our own mail order service and would be more than pleased to supply any of the stones listed.

Most Gemstones and Crystals, with just a few exceptions (eg Mother of Pearl), can be supplied in the form of Tumblestones. These are smooth, rounded stones, ideal as a Birthstone or as Healing Crystals. The nature of Mother of Pearl, and one or two others, prevents them being supplied as Tumblestones; however, we would be pleased to supply these in their natural form.

For further details - write to:
Rosewood,
P.O. Box 219. Huddersfield, West Yorkshire. HD2 2YT
E-mail enquiries to: **info@rosewood-gifts.co.uk**
Or why not visit our website for even more information
www.rosewood-gifts.co.uk

Other titles in the 'POWER FOR LIFE' series:

Discover your own Special Birthstone and the renowned Healing Powers of Crystals REF. (BK1) A look at Birthstones, personality traits and characteristics associated with each Sign of the Zodiac – plus a guide to the author's own unique range of Power Gems.

A Special Glossary of Healing Stones plus Birthstones REF. (BK2) An introduction to Crystal Healing, with an invaluable Glossary listing common ailments and suggesting combinations of Gemstones/Crystals.

Create a Wish Kit using a Candle, a Crystal and the Imagination of Your Mind REF. (BK3) 'The key to happiness is having dreams; the key to success is making dreams come true.' This book will help you achieve.

Gemstone & Crystal Elixirs – Potions for Love, Health, Wealth, Energy and Success REF. (BK4) An ancient form of 'magic', invoking super-natural powers. You won't believe the power you can get from a drink!

Crystal Pendulum for Dowsing REF. (BK5) An ancient knowledge for unlocking your Psychic Power, to seek out information not easily available by any other means. Contains easy-to-follow instructions.

How to Activate the Hidden Power in Gemstones and Crystals REF. (BK7) The key is to energise the thought using a crystal. The conscious can direct – but discover the real power. It's all in this book.

Astrology: The Secret Code REF. (BK8) In church it's called 'Myers Briggs typology'. In this book it's called 'psychological profiling'. If you read your horoscope, you need to read this to find your true birthstone.

Talismans, Charms and Amulets REF. (BK9) Making possible the powerful transformations which we would not normally feel empowered to do without a little extra help. Learn how to make a lucky talisman.

A Guide to the Mysteries surrounding Gemstones & Crystals REF. (BK10) Crystal healing, birthstones, crystal gazing, lucky talismans, elixirs, crystal dowsing, astrology, rune stones, amulets and rituals.

A Simple Guide to Gemstone & Crystal Power – a mystical A-Z of stones REF. (BK11) From Agate to Zircon, all you ever needed or wanted to know about the mystical powers of gemstones and crystals.

Change Your Life by Using the Most Powerful Crystal on Earth REF. (BK12) The most powerful crystal on earth can be yours. A book so disarmingly simple to understand, yet with a tremendous depth of knowledge.

All the above books are available from your local stockist,
or, if not, from the publisher.

NOTES

Welcome to the world of Rosewood

An extract from a 'thank- you' letter for one of my books.

"I realised just how much you really had indeed understood me and my need for direction and truly have allowed me the confidence and strength to know and believe I can achieve whatever I want in life"

If you like natural products, hand-crafted gifts including Gemstone jewellery, objects of natural beauty – the finest examples from Mother Nature, tinged with an air of Mystery – then we will not disappoint you. For those who can enjoy that feeling of connection with the esoteric nature of Gemstones and Crystals, then our 'Power for Life – Power Bracelets could be ideal for you. Each bracelet comes with its own guide explaining a way of thinking that's so powerful it will change your life and the information comes straight from the Bible. e.g. read Mark 11: 22

We regularly give inspirational talks on Crystal Power – fact or fiction? A captivating story about the world's fascination with natural gemstones and crystals and how the Placebo effect explains the healing power of gemstones and crystals – it's intriguing. And it's available on a CD

To see our full range of books, jewellery and gifts including CD's and DVD'S

Visit our web site - www.rosewood-gifts.co.uk

To see our latest videos go to 'You Tube' and type in Rosewood Gifts.